For Those That Find Themselves in Darkness

For Those That Find Themselves in Darkness

Cover design by Dionna Gary

ISBN - 978-1-7346304-0-4 (Paperback)
ISBN - 978-1-7346304-1-1 (Ebook)

They threw bricks;
you made a home.

They stole you from your homeland;
you made a culture of your own.

They threw you in the fire;
you would not be consumed.

They gave you darkness;
my love you bloomed.

Contents

GENESIS

Rooted Pain

My mother, grandmother, great grandmother
hand-delivered their depression down to me.
Their ignored pain trickled right into my blood,
dripping from the leaves of our family tree.

I remember my mother telling me
God could fix me as she burned, sizzled
and pressed her burdens down my river of hair.
Repeating over and over again,
God wouldn't give me more than I could bear.

My ancestor said she saw God
at the bottom of the River Jordan.
Wanted to be baptized with Jesus,
make it into the Promised Land.
Said she'd be washed of her sins,
so when she didn't come back
God had to understand.

Massa took my baby for the third time.
Ripped him from my limbs
and sold him down a river,
where he'll never know
who his true mama is.

Now he got me suckling
a white baby that ain't mine.
The only pleasure I get is knowing
that for a while, this black breast
will have this white baby
questioning who its real mama is.

God took my daughter's
daughter's daughter from her.
She keeps asking Him why.
Over a hundred years later,
and she has to feel the pain
of the tears I cried.
Now, she has that faraway look in her eye.
The same look
I had when I couldn't tell
my stolen children goodbye.

Head stuck under water,
devouring silent screams.
Can't even escape reality
through my dreams.
I tried talking to God,
but I'm getting no answer on my knees.

Tired of people asking
what's wrong with me,
when I don't even know myself.
I'm a black woman in America
so no one's concerned about my mental health.
Besides people will think I'm crazy,
and I can barely afford to seek help.

I'm tired of being in pain,
but I'm gonna keep fighting
with the strength of my foremothers
pumping through my veins.
Make sure that the cycle
of our family tree is forever changed.

Jezebel

There have been white women
who have historically lied
about being raped.
Black women
have historically been forced
to be quiet.

She knows her daughter has been raped
because she has been raped herself.
But the master of her great great grandmother
said she wanted it,
so she ignores and denies the same predator,
even believes she brought it upon herself.

Now she blames her daughter,
for displaying the same fast ways
that somehow invited the violence against her body.
I don't care what you do, just don't tell anybody.

How are we labeled the Jezebels
for existing in our own bodies,
while men parade around the Bible
not harming anybody,
but other men?
Who would've thought
being a black woman was a sin,
that invites and validates
all harm done to her.

How can you mistreat the same woman
who brings life into the universe?
And she should never have to prove her worth,
because she is worthy.
So your constant disrespect of her
will not deter me
from validating,
believing in,
and making her feel honored.
Because just like you,
I recognize her infinite power.

Eucharist

My body does not belong to me.
Their flesh crawling upon my flesh.
Holy Communion.
Take this bread and eat it.
What am I to do if I run out of loaves?

My body has been sacrificed.
Slaughtered to feed perceptive desires
of this jezebel.
I have allowed you to drink from my cup
freely.
Ain't my blood good enough?
I have filled your chalice and solo,
don't I taste good to you?

My body is not mine.
I have stained your tongue.
Drunkenly slipped into your tabernacle,
but you will not consecrate me.
The grapes from my vine
are now too sour for you.

My sweet manna,
unleavened,
will never be good enough
for heaven or earth.

MISSING WHILE BLACK

Today, they found my eyes
in a head that does not belong to me.
Yesterday, they found my teeth
in the mouth of a man twice my age.

I am a blind, toothless black boy.
They have eaten from my flesh
and left me to rot.

Yesterday I was kidnapped.
My body harvested and made ripe
for those in the market for buying black girls.
Tomorrow they won't find me.

I am a missing, dead black girl.
They have plucked at and eaten me
like a crow would a crop.

My face will not make the news.
No one will look for me, but my community.
Because what is rotten is thrown in the trash.
And though I am treasure, I will remain buried.

MOSES WAS BLACK

It has been dark for three days
you're no longer a slave
but they refuse to let you go
we celebrate Juneteenth
but they created Jim Crow

I made you as dark as night
so when they come at night
you'll blend into the trees
but I can still smell your berry flesh
swinging through the breeze

I swiped blood over the door
hoping that death would pass
I couldn't keep you in the house forever
so I dipped your feet in blood
hoping to protect you path
everybody called me crazy and even laughed
but I'm raising a black son in America
what other choice do I have

They would like to make you believe
that your darkness is a plague
drown you in a river of your own blood
but you're still breathing my love
even when they take your last breath
don't you ever stop breathing love

TROUBLED WATERS

My forefathers once told me
a man worth my tears
will never make me cry
but they have been baptized
with my mother's tears
as I wash their feet with my own
they bathe in the rain
falling from my sister's eyes
and wade in the water
flowing from my grandmother's

They think they can use our tears
to wash away their sins
but they have recreated Hurricane Katrina
destroyed our home,
drowned us
with no help from FEMA

AMERICAN DREAM

My forefathers have never loved me
they have only loved my flesh
for what it could produce for them
they do not love my foremothers
they only want their flesh
to eat their strange fruit

And since we are flesh of their flesh
our blood drips from our forefathers lips
and stains their hands
our bones used to pick their teeth

Bodies hanging from the same trees we come from

KISMET

My forefathers want their children to be blessed
when they have cursed so many
our birthright is their karma

They have spent their entire lives
running from themselves
trying to dodge what they have earned

My foremothers have tried to protect us
for they know only fools think
their earned misfortune is addressed to them

WAVES AT MIDNIGHT

My black don't rub off
capfuls of bleach
in my bath water
only left a ring
around the rosie
white privilege
is the plague
my coffee
is always black
drink up

Acid in pools
Boat rocking
Bodies on the ocean floor
Seasick
I will probably drown
because I am too afraid to swim
Noah's ark didn't float
40 days and 40 nights for this

This fear waded 400 years
Where do you lay your burdens
when you can't see the riverside?

BIRTH OF A WOMAN

You were brought here
through torn flesh
a mark left on your body
as a reminder of your first
birth

Stretch marks left on skin
that stretched to make
room for you

You will not remember
but your mother will

Your second birth
will leave a mark
on your soul

Born through a womb
that was always destined
to become too small for you

You will both
cry, scream, and shout
for two women
cannot occupy the same body

GENERATIONAL WEALTH

I'll always remember my mommy saying
I want you to be better than me
but I think she underestimated
how high she set the bar

As an adult I see every scar
that she has had to rub cocoa butter on
now I know what healing looks like
now I know the complexity of being every woman
and the simplicity of being your own woman

My dad made sure I loved my brown
and the crown
sitting on my head
made sure that I knew
there was nothing to dread
about the locs in my brothers and sisters' hair

He made sure I knew
the richness of my true history
explained the philosophy
used to demonize my black skin
taught me my blackness wasn't a sin
showed me that my greatest power
was within my pen

And if in my next lifetime
I get to be black a black woman again
I would choose them

HERSTORY

The bodies that survived
ships
plantations
sells to the highest bidder
Jim Crow
Civil Rights

The hands that ached
over kitchen stove
brushing white hair
scrubbing floors
taking care of white and black children

The wombs that were invaded
with speculums
uninvited seed
abrupt force
to birth nations

The backs that curved
over washtub
in hot sun
to get you outta yo cotton pickin' mind

The feet that ran
in dark woods
from baton swinging,
firehose spraying
men raping
to get you to freedom

Whom shall we fear?

19

WILDERNESS

Y
O
U
W
A
N
N
A
put my pain on display,
disrespect my body,
and humiliate me as a

lesson about what being Black
whipped me in front of my
of God in them. Slapped
my beating, just to inform
and would be next. You
hanging from a tree. You
the street. You beat and
You tear gas protesters
to ask not to be killed.
shall not kill? You grad-
gang to prison industrial
continues to be caught
criminalized, placed on
for deserving our own
my black brothers and
your TV screens. I will
murdered and brutalized
just for sport. Just as a re-
er been safe, that you will
make sure we remember
free. Your racism has shape
itself as progress. I don't
or anything that'll help you
everything my black ancestors

in America gets you. You
community, to instill the fear
on a badge and broadcast
my family that they could
strung me up and left me
left my bleeding body in
jailed the freedom riders.
who have the audacity
What happened to thou
uated from the chain
complex. Our genocide
on tape, just for us to be
trial, and found guilty
public execution. Take
sisters' murders off
not be desensitized to
black folks you prey on
minder that we have nev-
come in our homes and
that we have never been
shifted and tried to disguise
want your fake diversity,
ease your white guilt. I want
built...

21

```
T
H          A              D
I          B              E
N          O              A
K          U              T
N'         T              H
```

on my birthday. Lord knows I wanna give up in the worst way, but today is the one day I'm supposed to be happy. Blowing out candles, making memories and laughing, but I'm only laughing to keep from crying, cause on the inside I feel like dying. And how could God curse me with another year? When I prayed so damn hard not to make it here. It's messed up that my biggest fear is more life without a stable career, and I can't stop comparing myself to my peers, and damn I don't wanna hear another person tell me it'll get better.

If better wasn't me drowning from the stormy weather, there ain't no sunshine warm enough to pull me together, cause damn I was supposed to have it all together by now. But I'm stuck on my mama's couch and bills haven't stopped since I got out of college with a degree that hasn't done me any good yet. But I went into debt, and I don't have the net worth they promised would come with this piece of paper. And I've never been a hater, but what do they have that I don't? Hold on, wait. Now it's time to eat the cake, but like Anna Mae, I don't want it. I hate all the negative reflection brought on by this moment.

As I eat too much icing, I'm thinking about my ex, and how all the sex wasn't good enough, to distract me from all the time I've wasted. I thought I was patient, but everybody's getting married and having babies, while I'm stuck with men who are always afraid of commitment. But I guess I'm no different, cause I can't even admit that I have become the embodiment of what I'm attracting. And I've never been into acting, but I deserve an Oscar. Cause I'm smiling and celebrating like the waves of my depression aren't threatening to destroy this whole party. Forgive me I'm sorry, I said I wouldn't cry. But I don't think I can tell the world, or myself, another lie...

AIN'T NO SUNSHINE

I have searched for you
in everyone but you
no wonder I could never find you
and if ye seeks
ye shall find
wondering if I'll ever find you
cause I've been lost
I have paid the cost
so why am I still broken

Buried myself within myself
I will die here
I don't wanna die here
is this what hell feels like
I would scream
but the soil in my throat
will not allow me
I will decompose here
if I am not careful

But I am still searching
for you
sun has not shone here
in the last 100 days
I thought I could bloom in darkness

I am afraid
there's no air here
my lungs will collapse soon
leaving me here lifeless.

What if I die in this place?

THE LAST PRAYER

I am below the bottom
reaching for an early grave
the last prayer to leave my lips
was soaked in death
drowning in suicidal thoughts
how could I ask God for this?

I breathe easy
at the thought of sleep
eternally
maybe
He'll give it to me
this time

sweet relief
I can feel the Grim Reaper
smiling
waiting for this gift

unwanted gifts
should be able to be returned
why do I have to keep
what I do not want
I did not ask God for this

KEPT WOMAN

Today I will be honest with myself
today I acknowledge
that I have been coping
keeping busy
to keep my mind
off of the pain you brought me
and that's a shame
cause mama didn't raise me
to be a kept woman

PARDON ME

Mama always said
the devil sends a counterfeit
but I didn't care
as long as I got to choose the man
I wanted to sin with

And of course I repented
but this is the seventh time
and I feel at some point there's a line
where God won't forgive me
and I'm missing
out on all of the blessings He said He'd give me
if I'd just be obedient

But obedience is the only ingredient
that doesn't mix with my life of sin
and I know I said I wouldn't do it again
but just one more time
won't hurt nobody
and I'll be done for good
and I know the last time
God said He understood
but damn sleeping with the devil
feels so good

Now mama keeps telling me
to stop letting them bite my apple
but what's wrong with a little sample
especially when I know
we're both descendants of Eve
and since the apple doesn't fall far from the tree
I guess this was destined

I'm trying to learn my lesson
replant the seeds
and pull myself from the pit of my flesh
because I'm really starting to burn
and I know this is what I earned
but can you please let me back in the garden
I know you said you'd forgive me seventy times seven
so I'm begging for your pardon

POT OF GOLD

I wanna feel love
but to do that I have to understand pain
I wanna dance with you under rainbows
but I have to respect the rain
I wanna suck on the sweet sugar
but I can't ignore the deep roots of the cane

You and I are as bittersweet
as the taste of your dark chocolate skin
on my tongue
and yes we had fun
but let's face it we're not as young
as we used to be

And yes we have history
but neither of us can solve the mystery
of why this love thing always has to hurt
we've shouted down walls
fought our families
and contemplated poison
just to make this work

But we're no Romeo and Juliet
and while I acknowledge that
I'm not ready to let this go yet
because I think I still
no, I know I will always love you
but my voice isn't as strong as Whitney's
and where I was once so sure
I now need convincing
and damn this is the part
where you always go missing

Now I look stupid
cause what mama said
has always been right
but damn I still wanna fight
for you

Cause you're all I know
we've hurt each other so many times
but I never thought you'd stoop so low
so now I gotta go
and give everyone the satisfaction
of I told you so

But woah
this was supposed to be about love
but it ain't never been blue skies
without the rain
which is why to be with me
my next love will have to understand
my pain

First Things First

And how am I supposed to
let someone new into my body
when my sacred places
have only been explored by you
when the curves of my body
curve into your body
so perfectly
Lord have mercy
here come the flashbacks

Memories of the first time
I let you touch me
how lovely
it would've been for you to be
the first, last and only

If only
you would've taken care of my heart
like you did my body
cause now I can't fathom another body
touching me but yours

FENG SHUI

My body is my home.
I invited you in
you spent the night
and then you suddenly lived here

                    I allowed you to redecorate
                    make yourself feel at home
                    gave you a place to rest
                    what need was there to roam

But you left me all alone
so many nights you didn't come home
now I want you gone

                    You've packed your things
                    yet your presence still lingers
                    the space I made for you is now empty
                    although I was never for sale
                    you were supposed to buy, not rent me
                    how did you manage to move out so quickly

Then comes the fear
this is my home
but pieces of you are still left my dear
it's been a year
and I still don't know how
I'm going to invite someone new here

VACANCY

I spilled my feelings on the floor.
You stepped on them,
instead of helping me clean them up.
So, I left them there
hoping to track your footprints.
I followed them to a stranger's house.
It's clear that love don't live here anymore.
Maybe it never did.

MONA'S CURSE

You never saw me
never saw me neatly fold into myself
to make beautiful origami
just to become art for you

But I never allowed you to touch me
to feel the intricate textures
to understand the patterns
that make me a masterpiece
and you never tried
because what was pleasing to your eyesight
was all that mattered

So I framed myself
became a work of art
no one could touch

Weeping Willow

I walked to my family tree
but it had been uprooted
turned on its side
a gaping hole where it once stood
its connection to earth dangling
reaching, stretching
trying to find its way back home

leaves are scattered and dying
no longer breathing life into my world
weeping

I knew this day was coming
the deep roots
were slowly bursting through the grass
one by one
but I ignored it
tried to cover it with soil
until it pulled itself from its home

Who am I now?

PROMISED LAND

For Those That Find Themselves in Darkness

I became a flower today
freed myself and bloomed in darkness
how wonderful it felt
to blossom in my darkest hour

Rooted in good ground
I will always bear fruit
I am reflections of moons, stars
and all things that shine
in the absence of light

I am petals, stems and soil
I am mustard seeds of faith
I am sugar sweet nectar
and chocolate flowers
sprinkling my cocoa fragrance
for those who know that
darkness births beautiful things

I am growth
that does not need to be seen
to be beautiful

OLIVE BRANCH

Yes the tree fell
in a quiet place
on solid ground
remove your sandals Moses
feel the history rich soil
on which you stand

irrational fears of September
branches were meant to break
leaves were designed to die
the tree was always destined to fall

but March is always coming
there's an olive branch after every storm
wipe your tears
does spring not grant growth?

your roots were not damaged
can't you hear granny now
with a smile in her voice
chile that tree gone be alright
rebirth is in your nature

MARK 4:39

Peace be still running around
Peace
be
still
I'm trying to find you
Peace
be still
the storm is calm now

Time to undress my burdens
peel the lifelong
pain from my body
scrub away the hurt
let the tears cleanse me
for once my nakedness
not a reflection of shame
the moments before Eve bit that apple
rolling around in my own Eden

This what they sing about?
Clap they hands to?
Dance on a Friday night in a juke joint to?
This what joy feel like?
This what comes in the mornin'?

WOMAN

And what if I am not wife
if I am not mother
if my breasts never overflow with milk
if my vagina only stops bleeding
when time tells it to

And what if these breasts
this uterus
this body
decides to self-destruct
leaving only scars behind

Will I suddenly become man?

If I have only broken ribs
and not sprouted from them
does that make me any less Eve?

LONG STORY SHORT

I couldn't make you heal the open wounds
that happened before me
oh how I wish I could change the story
that was bound to destroy our story
but I can't heal everybody

as a matter of fact
I'm only responsible for healing myself
and I guess
that's the most important thing we taught me

Mason Jar

If only our hearts
could have broken at the same time
but they were never truly connected
while I was searching
for blood colored Band-Aids
doing everything I could to hide the pain
you were finding ways
to shatter what was already broken
continually poking
with words spoken
to make me believe
it was my fault
poured so much saline
in my wounds
I damn near became a pillar of salt

But I refused to let my heart harden
used the tears I cried to water my garden
made the holes in my heart
a home to plant my flowers

BROKEN GLASS

Now you seek me
                        to heal your broken pieces
   want to avoid all the lessons
                        heartbreak teaches
      but the aisle
                        for blood colored Band-Aids
            does not actually exist
and I cannot help you fix
                        what I did not break
and there are consequences
                        for every mistake
      but it wasn't a mistake
                        I had to be pushed
      because I would not move
                        on my own
now I've used the stones
                        you threw to break our glass house
      to build a new home

PARTING GIFT

As if I should worship you
for finally offering to love me
when my love at your feet
was not good enough

You kick and scream
because how dare I
not accept an unwanted gift
but my love, what gift?

A last minute love
is not worthy of me

SPILLED MILK

I don't have the heart to tell you
  I don't love you anymore
    it happened gradually
      then all at once
        like the feelings gathered in my chest
          and the remains poured from my eyes
            the last time I would ever cry over you

An Ode to D'Angelo

How does it feel
to wear the skin I shed?
You now grieve
for what I have already buried.
You hold the ashes
to the bridge I watched burn.
You cry over spilled milk
that has long been cleaned up.
Your delayed pain does not move me
just as my instant pain did not move you.

And I'd give myself over again
just to become so lost in you
that I find myself
that I find a peace so deep
that my deepest mistakes
cannot disturb me
because I am not ashamed
to say that I have given
what I did not have
that I have loved foolishly
that I gave to you
what a mother would her child
when I did not birth you

-REST IN PEACE

DEFINED

I am light when there is no light.
I am sunshine in the midst of the storm.
I am beautifully complex.
I am words to this poem.
I am tall mountains; I am low valleys.
I am tears of joy and sadness.

I am nourishment for my own soul.
Because of me, I am made whole
from the half-truths and full lies
that tell me I am less than woman,
if I am just woman.

DUST

What becomes you?
The strength of your thick hair?
The steadfastness of your long spine?
The grace of your thick thighs?

The beautiful prayers your mother
sprinkled over your sleeping mind
My child, do you not recognize your own beauty?
The universe will go to war for you.

May you kiss your reflection and see God.
Your toes have touched good ground.
You shall not return to the earth empty.

PHOENIX

And maybe I let things go too far
but love is not only defined by what you want
but by discovering what you do not
and yes I was scorned
but I had to feel the heat for myself

I'm not afraid to admit
that the pain was so deep
I tried to bury us
because really a part of me died
but I'd die a million times
just to rebirth this woman

Ayesha Ewing is a poet, storyteller and writer. She is best known for her annual #makingblackherstory campaign that explores and celebrates her African American roots, through poetry shared every day of Black History Month. Born and raised in St. Louis, Ayesha currently lives and works in Southern California.

www.ingramcontent.com/pod-product-compliance
Lightning Source LLC
Chambersburg PA
CBHW031616040426
42452CB00006B/552